cereal
sweets
& Treats

WRITTEN & PHOTOGRAPHED

BY Jessica segarra

GIBBS SMITH
TO ENRICH AND INSPIRE HUMANKIND

contents

introduction

THERE ARE FEW THINGS IN THIS WORLD that I love more than cereal. I love the crunch of the cereal and the sweet milk that's left behind. Growing up, my family would be eating spaghetti around the dinner table, and you would find me with a gigantic bowl of cereal instead.

Even as an adult, I will choose a bowl of cereal over almost any other dinner option served to me. I can happily eat it for breakfast, lunch, dinner, and even as a snack. Sadly as we grow up, all those sugar laden cereals we enjoyed as a kid turn into forbidden fruit. Instead of reaching for that box of Cookie Crisps, we go for the sensible, grown up option. I am on a mission to change that.

Once I got married and started baking, I discovered all the ways I could turn my favorite cereals into desserts. At first it was just the traditional recipes, like regular marshmallow treats and trail mixes. Then I started branching out into things like Fruity Pebbles Macarons and Cap'n Crunch Milkshakes—and my world as I knew it changed.

I started my blog (www.thenovicechefblog.com) in 2008 and slowly shared some of my favorite cereal creations there. The impact they made was incredible and I could not believe the feedback they were receiving. I knew right then and there that I would write a cookbook all about desserts made with cereal and here we are, years down the road with that pipe dream now a reality.

This cookbook is a love letter to sugary cereal and to all the cereal lovers out there. I hope you enjoy making the recipes as much as I enjoyed dreaming them up!

EQUIPMENT

Candy Thermometer. A candy thermometer is a special thermometer for high temperatures when cooking candy. It is usually glass and attaches to the side of your pot.

Food Processor. A food processor is an important tool in a lot of the recipes found in this cookbook. Many recipes need the cereal to be powdered, without any lumps remaining. This is easily achieved with a few seconds in a food processor.

Ice Cream Maker. There is only one recipe where an ice cream maker is required, but it is one of my personal favorites. There are many different types of ice cream makers and any kind will do.

Double Boiler. When you are cooking or melting certain ingredients, a double boiler is required. If you do not have one, a double boiler can easily be made with a saucepan and a heatproof bowl that can sit on top.

Electric Mixer. While not required, they sure do make beautiful buttercreams and save your arm from a world of pain! Whether it's a stand mixer or a hand mixer, either will be helpful in a number of recipes.

Bars

Fruity Pebbles
Marshmallow Treats

FOR THOSE OF US WHO HAVE A SWEET TOOTH as big as our butts, these are the dessert you have been waiting for all your life. With a combination of the traditional marshmallowy goodness and sugary Fruity Pebbles, your sweet tooth will go into overload.

4 tablespoons unsalted butter

1 (10-ounce) bag mini marshmallows

6 cups Fruity Pebbles

Grease an 8 x 8-inch pan and set aside.

In a large nonstick stock pot, melt butter over medium-high heat. Add marshmallows and stir until completely melted. Remove from heat and fold in Fruity Pebbles until well coated.

Transfer mixture to prepared pan and spread evenly using a buttered spatula. When cooled, cut into squares and serve immediately. Can be stored in an airtight container, but are best served fresh.

Makes 9 treats

Espresso
Cheerios Bars

CHEERIOS MAY USUALLY HANG OUT WITH MILK, but their real favorite flavor pairing is espresso. With a little peanut butter to deepen the flavor, these Espresso Cheerios Bars are perfect when served with your morning coffee.

1 cup corn syrup

1/2 cup packed brown sugar

2 tablespoons instant espresso powder

1/2 cup creamy peanut butter

4 cups Cinnamon Cheerios

3 cups Chocolate Cheerios

Grease an 8 x 8-inch pan and set aside.

In a large nonstick stock pot, bring corn syrup, brown sugar, and espresso powder to a boil, stirring constantly. Remove from heat and stir in peanut butter. Fold in both flavors of Cheerios until well coated.

Transfer mixture to prepared pan and spread evenly using a buttered spatula. When cooled, cut into squares and serve immediately. Can be stored in an airtight container, but are best served fresh.

Makes 9 Bars

Cake Batter
Rice Krispies Treats

CAKE BATTER HAS BEEN A HUGE FLAVOR TREND LATELY, and not being one to sit by and watch a trend go by, you just have to try some Cake Batter Rice Krispies Treats!

5 tablespoons unsalted butter

1 (10-ounce) bag mini marshmallows

1/3 cup yellow cake mix

5 cups Rice Krispies

1/4 cup sprinkles

Grease an 8 x 8-inch pan and set aside.

In a large nonstick stock pot, melt butter over medium-high heat. Add marshmallows and stir until completely melted. Stir in cake mix. Remove from heat and fold in Rice Krispies and sprinkles until well coated.

Transfer mixture to prepared pan and spread evenly using a buttered spatula. When cooled, cut into squares and serve immediately. Can be stored in an airtight container, but are best served fresh.

Makes 9 treats

Lucky Charms
Milk Bars

DON'T LET THE TERM "MILK BARS" CONFUSE YOU, these are sweeter than a bowl full of candy. With the marshmallows in Lucky Charms and the marshmallows in the recipe, you will be flying high on sugar all day long.

1/2 cup unsalted butter

1 (10-ounce) bag mini marshmallows

1/3 cup instant dry milk

5 cups Lucky Charms

Grease a 9 x 13-inch pan and set aside.

In a large nonstick stock pot, melt butter over medium-high heat. Add marshmallows and stir until completely melted. Stir in dry milk. Remove from heat and fold in Lucky Charms until well coated.

Transfer mixture to prepared pan and spread evenly using a buttered spatula. When cooled, cut into squares and serve immediately. Can be stored in an airtight container, but are best served fresh.

Makes 12 bars

PUMPKIN
CHEERIOS BARS

A BUTTERY CHEERIOS CRUST AND CREAMY PUMPKIN LAYER make these irresistible. With these scrumptious bars, you will want to enjoy pumpkin year round!

4 cups Cinnamon Cheerios

1/2 cup sugar

1/2 cup unsalted butter, melted

1 (15-ounce) can pumpkin

1 (14-ounce) can sweetened condensed milk

2 eggs

1 teaspoon cinnamon

1/2 teaspoon nutmeg

1/2 teaspoon salt

Powdered sugar, for garnish

Preheat oven to 350 degrees. Grease a 9 x 13-inch pan and set aside.

Add Cheerios, sugar, and melted butter to the bowl of a food processor and process until a ball of dough forms. Using a buttered spatula, press dough evenly into prepared pan and set aside.

In a large bowl, whisk together pumpkin, condensed milk, eggs, cinnamon, nutmeg, and salt. Pour pumpkin mixture on top of crust and spread evenly.

Bake for 40–45 minutes, until center is set. Remove from oven and let cool completely. Cut into squares and dust the tops with powdered sugar. Serve immediately or store in refrigerator until ready to serve.

MAKES 12 BARS

Cocoa Pebbles
Peanut Butter Treats

PEANUT BUTTER AND CHOCOLATE have always been best friends, but they were totally meant to be together in these Cocoa Pebbles Peanut Butter Treats. If you are looking for an extra-sugar rush, try dipping these in a chocolate fondue!

4 tablespoons unsalted butter

4 cups mini marshmallows

1/2 cup creamy peanut butter

4 cups Cocoa Pebbles

Grease an 8 x 8-inch pan and set aside.

In a large nonstick stock pot, melt butter over medium-high heat. Add marshmallows and stir until completely melted. Stir in peanut butter. Remove from heat and fold in Cocoa Pebbles until well coated.

Transfer mixture to prepared pan and spread evenly using a buttered spatula. When cooled, cut into squares and serve immediately. Can be stored in an airtight container, but are best served fresh.

Makes 9 treats

GOLDEN GRAHAMS
S'mores

SITTING AROUND A CAMPFIRE is no longer the only way to fill that s'mores craving! These Golden Grahams S'mores are the perfect way to scratch that itch when it's too hot to hold a marshmallow over the fire.

1/2 cup unsalted butter

1 (16-ounce) bag mini marshmallows

1 (12-ounce) box Golden Grahams

4 ounces dark chocolate, roughly chopped

Grease an 8 x 8-inch pan and set aside.

In a large nonstick stock pot, melt butter over medium-high heat. Add marshmallows and stir until completely melted. Remove from heat and fold in Golden Grahams until well coated.

Transfer mixture to prepared pan and spread evenly using a buttered spatula. When cooled, cut into squares.

In a small microwave-safe bowl, microwave chocolate for 1 minute and stir. If not completely melted, continue to heat in 15 second intervals, stirring after each until smooth.

Drizzle squares with melted chocolate and serve immediately.

Makes 9 Bars

Brown Butter Rice Krispies Treats

WE ALL KNOW AND LOVE the traditional gooey marshmallow treats. And why shouldn't we? They are prefect in every way—except they are missing brown butter! Browning the butter adds a whole new nutty level of flavor to this traditional treat that is truly earth shattering.

1 cup unsalted butter

1 (16-ounce) bag mini marshmallows

1/2 teaspoon salt

8 cups Rice Krispies

Grease a 9 x 13-inch pan and set aside.

In a large nonstick stock pot, melt butter over medium-high heat. Cook, stirring occasionally, until butter turns a deep golden color and you see a few dark flecks. Add the marshmallows and salt, and stir until marshmallows are completely melted. Remove from heat and fold in Rice Krispies until well coated.

Transfer mixture to prepared pan and spread evenly using a buttered spatula. When cooled, cut into squares and serve immediately. Can be stored in an airtight container, but are best served fresh.

Makes 12 Treats

cakes, cupcakes, & muffins

ALL-Bran APPLe COFFEE CAKE

COFFEE CAKE IS A TRADITION that should be honored and repeated. No brunch table is set without a coffee cake as the centerpiece. This All-Bran Apple Coffee Cake is everything you love about the traditional coffee cake, just with a special cereal twist.

$1^1/2$ cups crushed All-Bran Flakes, divided

$1^1/4$ cups sugar, divided

$1^1/2$ teaspoons cinnamon, divided

4 tablespoons unsalted butter, melted

$1^1/2$ cups flour

2 teaspoons baking powder

$1/2$ teaspoon baking soda

$1/2$ teaspoon nutmeg

$1/2$ teaspoon salt

$1/2$ cup unsalted butter, room temperature

2 eggs

1 teaspoon vanilla extract

$1/2$ cup applesauce

$1/2$ cup milk

3 medium apples, peeled and diced

Preheat oven to 350 degrees. Grease a 9 x 13-inch pan and set aside.

In a small mixing bowl, mix together $1/2$ cup crushed All-Bran Flakes, $1/4$ cup sugar, and $1/2$ teaspoon cinnamon. Pour in melted butter, stirring until crumbly. Set aside.

In a medium bowl, whisk together remaining crushed All-Bran Flakes, flour, baking powder, baking soda, remaining cinnamon, nutmeg, and salt. Set aside.

In a large bowl, cream together butter and remaining sugar until light and fluffy. Beat in eggs, vanilla, and applesauce. Add in flour mixture alternating with milk, until smooth. Fold in apples and transfer to prepared pan. Sprinkle evenly with crumbled topping.

Bake for 35 minutes, or until a toothpick inserted in the center comes out clean. Cool and cut into squares.

Makes 12 servings

CHEX
Brownies

IF YOU ARE LOOKING FOR A TWIST on the classic brownie, these chocolate bombs are for you. With a layer of crunchy Rice Chex and chocolate chips on the bottom, these are sure to satisfy any chocolate craving!

2 cups Rice Chex

1/2 cup semisweet chocolate chips

1/2 cup flour

1/3 cup cocoa powder

1/2 teaspoon salt

1/2 cup unsalted butter, room temperature

1 cup sugar

2 eggs

1/3 cup vegetable oil

1 teaspoon vanilla extract

Preheat oven to 325 degrees.

Grease an 8 x 8-inch pan. Spread Rice Chex and chocolate chips in an even layer in bottom of pan and set aside.

In a medium bowl, whisk together flour, cocoa powder, and salt. Set aside.

In a large bowl or stand mixer, cream together butter and sugar. Add eggs, oil, and vanilla. Whisk in flour mixture until well combined.

Carefully pour batter over Chex layer and smooth the top. Bake for 35–40 minutes, or until a toothpick inserted in the center comes out with just a few crumbs on it.

Cool and cut into squares. Serve immediately, or store in an airtight container for up to 3 days.

Makes 9 Brownies

Fruit Loops
Cupcakes

WITH A BURST OF FRUITY FLAVOR AND DENSE CAKE, these Fruit Loops Cupcakes are a sensation. By adding a few Fruit Loops to the top of each cupcake, these are sure to be a show stopper.

1/2 cup milk

1 cup Fruit Loops

1 1/4 cups flour

1 teaspoon baking powder

1/2 teaspoon baking soda

1/2 teaspoon salt

2 eggs

3/4 cup sugar

1 teaspoon vanilla extract

1/2 cup vegetable oil

Frosting

3/4 cup unsalted butter, room temperature

1 teaspoon vanilla extract

1 3/4 cups powdered sugar

1/2 cup finely ground Fruit Loops

Preheat oven to 350 degrees. Line a muffin pan with cupcake liners and set aside.

In a medium bowl, stir together milk and fruit loops. Let soak for 20 minutes, stirring occasionally. Strain out cereal and discard. Set cereal milk aside.

In a medium bowl, whisk together flour, baking powder, baking soda, and salt. Set aside. In a large bowl, beat together eggs, sugar, and vanilla. Add half of flour mixture and oil, stirring until combined. Add remaining flour mixture and cereal milk, stirring until fully combined.

Divide batter evenly among muffin cups, filling 3/4 full. Bake for 16–18 minutes, or until a toothpick inserted in the center comes out clean. Let cool in muffin pan for 10 minutes and transfer to a wire rack to cool completely before frosting.

In a stand mixer, cream butter and vanilla together. Add powdered sugar, beating until light and fluffy, about 2 minutes. Slowly add ground Fruit Loops, scraping down the sides and bottom of the bowl as needed. If needed, add 1 teaspoon of milk at a time until the desired buttercream consistency is reached. Spoon frosting into a pastry bag with a large tip opening and pipe onto cooled cupcakes. Store in an airtight container until ready to serve. If no milk was added to the frosting, the cupcakes do not need to be refrigerated.

Makes 12 cupcakes

LUCKY CHARMS CUPCAKES

A DELICIOUS LUCKY CHARMS SCENTED CAKE is topped with a dollop of marshmallow frosting in these Lucky Charms Cupcakes. Use Lucky Charms as sprinkles on top of the cupcakes for an extra pop of color.

$1/2$ cup milk

1 cup Lucky Charms

$1 1/4$ cups flour

1 teaspoon baking powder

$1/2$ teaspoon baking soda

$1/2$ teaspoon salt

2 eggs

$3/4$ cup sugar

1 teaspoon vanilla extract

$1/2$ cup vegetable oil

Frosting

2 egg whites

$1/2$ cup sugar

$1/4$ teaspoon cream of tartar

2 teaspoons vanilla extract

Preheat oven to 350 degrees. Line a muffin pan with cupcake liners and set aside.

In a medium bowl, stir together milk and Lucky Charms. Let soak for 20 minutes, stirring occasionally. Strain out cereal and discard. Set cereal milk aside.

In a medium bowl, whisk together flour, baking powder, baking soda, and salt. Set aside. In a large bowl, beat together eggs, sugar, and vanilla. Add half of flour mixture and oil, stirring until combined. Add remaining flour mixture and cereal milk, stirring until fully combined.

Divide batter evenly among muffin cups, filling $3/4$ full. Bake for 16–18 minutes, or until a toothpick inserted in the center comes out clean. Let cool in muffin pan for 10 minutes and transfer to a wire rack to cool completely before frosting.

Place egg whites, sugar, and cream of tartar in a double boiler over medium-high heat. Whisk egg white mixture constantly until sugar has dissolved and the whites are foamy and warm to the touch.

Transfer egg whites to a stand mixer fitted with the whisk attachment. Beat egg whites until stiff, glossy peaks form. Add vanilla and mix until combined. Spoon frosting into a pastry bag with a large tip opening and pipe onto cooled cupcakes; serve immediately.

Makes 12 cupcakes

Cocoa Puffs Cupcakes

WITH A DENSE CHOCOLATE CAKE as its base and a tower of Cocoa Puffs buttercream on top, this cupcake will quickly soar to the top of your favorites!

1 cup flour

$^1/_2$ cup cocoa powder

1 teaspoon baking powder

$^1/_2$ teaspoon baking soda

$^1/_2$ teaspoon salt

2 eggs

1 cup sugar

$^1/_2$ cup sour cream

$^1/_4$ cup vegetable oil

1 tablespoon vanilla extract

Frosting

$^1/_2$ cup unsalted butter, room temperature

1 teaspoon vanilla extract

1 cup powdered sugar

$^1/_2$ cup finely ground Cocoa Puffs

1–2 teaspoons milk, if needed

Preheat oven to 350 degrees. Line a muffin pan with cupcake liners and set aside.

In a medium bowl, whisk together flour, cocoa powder, baking powder, baking soda, and salt. Set aside.

In a large bowl, whisk together eggs, sugar, sour cream, oil, and vanilla. Fold in the dry ingredients, mixing until just combined.

Divide batter evenly among muffin cups, filling $^3/_4$ full. Bake for 16–18 minutes, or until a toothpick inserted in the center comes out clean. Transfer cupcakes to a wire rack and let cool completely.

In a stand mixer, beat the butter until creamy. Mix in the vanilla on low. Beat in powdered sugar and then add the ground Cocoa Puffs, $^1/_4$ cup at a time.

If buttercream is too thick, add 1 teaspoon of cold milk at a time until desired consistency is reached. Spoon frosting into a pastry bag with a large tip opening and pipe onto cooled cupcakes; serve immediately.

Makes 12 cupcakes

orange Frosted Flakes
Glazed Muffins

WHAT IS THE DIFFERENCE between a cupcake and a muffin? One is dessert and the other is breakfast! These Orange Frosted Flakes Glazed Muffins are the perfect example of that mind-set. With the addition of the orange glaze, you will never miss the buttercream usually found on a cupcake!

3/4 cup flour

1 teaspoon baking powder

1/2 teaspoon baking soda

1/4 teaspoon salt

4 tablespoons unsalted butter,
　　room temperature

1/2 cup sugar

1 egg

1 teaspoon vanilla extract

1/2 cup applesauce

1/4 cup milk

1 teaspoon orange zest

3/4 cup crushed Frosted Flakes

Glaze

1 cup powdered sugar

1 tablespoon fresh orange juice

Preheat oven to 350 degrees. Prepare muffin pan with cupcake liners or grease with butter.

In a medium bowl, whisk together flour, baking powder, baking soda, and salt. Set aside.

In a large bowl, cream together butter and sugar. Add egg and vanilla. Add half of flour mixture and applesauce, stirring until combined. Add remaining flour mixture, milk, and zest, stirring until combined. Fold in crushed Frosted Flakes.

Divide batter evenly among muffin cups, filling 3/4 full. Bake for 14–16 minutes, or until a toothpick inserted in the center comes out with just a few crumbs on it. Transfer muffins to a wire rack and let cool completely.

In a small bowl, whisk together powdered sugar and orange juice until smooth. Drizzle over top of muffins and serve immediately.

Makes 12 muffins

Cinnamon Toast Crunch Muffins

LOOKING FOR ANOTHER WAY to have your Cinnamon Toast Crunch in the morning? Try out these Cinnamon Toast Crunch Muffins for a perfect on-the-go breakfast!

3/4 cup flour

1/2 cup finely ground Cinnamon Toast Crunch

1 teaspoon cinnamon

3/4 teaspoon baking powder

1/4 teaspoon baking soda

1/4 teaspoon salt

1 egg

1/4 cup sugar

1/4 cup packed brown sugar

1/2 cup applesauce

1 teaspoon vanilla extract

1/4 cup vegetable oil

1/4 cup milk

Preheat oven to 350 degrees. Prepare muffin pan with cupcake liners or grease with butter.

In a medium bowl, whisk together flour, ground Cinnamon Toast Crunch, cinnamon, baking powder, baking soda, and salt. Set aside.

In a large bowl, whisk together egg, sugar, and brown sugar. Mix in applesauce and vanilla. Add half of flour mixture and vegetable oil, stirring until combined. Add remaining flour mixture and milk, stirring until combined.

Divide batter evenly among muffin cups, filling 3/4 full. Bake for 15–17 minutes, or until a toothpick inserted in the center comes out with just a few crumbs on it.

Let cool in muffin pan for 10 minutes and serve warm.

Makes 12 muffins

candies

Reese's Puffs Peanut Butter Truffles

WHILE SOME TRUFFLES MAY BE A PAIN TO CREATE, these little balls of sugar are a breeze to make. With just a few minutes you can create a delicious chocolate peanut butter treat that will please everyone!

2 cups Reese's Puffs

1/4 cup creamy peanut butter

6 ounces white chocolate, roughly chopped

Line a large baking sheet with parchment paper and set aside.

In a food processor, pulse Reese's Puffs and peanut butter together until a dough forms and there are no lumps left. Roll dough into 1-inch balls and place onto prepared baking sheet. Chill balls in the freezer for 15 minutes.

In a medium microwave-safe bowl, microwave chocolate for 1 minute and stir. If not completely melted, microwave in 15 second intervals, stirring after each until smooth.

Dip balls into melted chocolate using toothpicks or a fork. Return to baking sheet and sprinkle tops with crushed Reese's Puffs for garnish, if desired.

Let truffles coating harden on the counter for 1 hour or in the refrigerator for 20 minutes. Store in an airtight container for up to 3 days.

Makes 18 truffles

WHITE CHOCOLATE
TRIX BARK

WHILE THIS LOOKS LIKE A DESSERT MADE FOR KIDS, it's so good you won't want to share it with any little grabby fingers! The bright colors draw you in, but you stay for the fruity white chocolate flavors.

11 ounces white chocolate chips

1 1/2 cups Trix, divided

Line a large baking sheet with parchment paper and set aside.

Pulse 1/2 cup Trix in a food processor until powdered. Set aside.

In a medium microwave-safe bowl, microwave chocolate for 1 minute and stir. If not completely melted, microwave in 15 second intervals, stirring after each until smooth.

Pour half of the chocolate onto prepared baking sheet. Cover chocolate with powdered Trix, leaving a 1/2-inch border around the edges. Carefully pour the remaining chocolate on top, using the back of a spoon to spread to the edges. Sprinkle remaining 1 cup of Trix over the top of the chocolate and press gently to make sure the cereal sticks.

Chill in refrigerator for 30 minutes, or until hardened, break into pieces and serve immediately, or store in an airtight container for up to 3 days.

Makes 10–12 pieces

candied cheerios
chex mix

EVERYBODY SERVES CHEX MIX, but why not surprise everyone with Candied Cheerios Chex Mix? While still having all the traditional flavors, this Chex mix changes the game with a sweet, crunchy candy coating.

4 cups Rice Chex

4 cups Dulce De Leche Cheerios

1 cup sliced almonds

1/2 cup unsalted butter

1 cup sugar

1 cup light corn syrup

Line a large baking sheet with parchment paper and set aside.

In a large bowl, toss together Rice Chex, Cheerios, and almonds. Set aside.

In a medium saucepan, melt butter. Whisk in sugar and corn syrup. Cook, stirring occasionally, until a candy thermometer reaches 235 degrees (or the soft-ball stage).

Remove from heat and pour over cereal mixture, tossing to coat. Transfer to prepared baking sheet and spread into an even layer. Let cool completely and then break into clusters. Store in an airtight container for up to 5 days.

Quick Tip: Feel free to change up the ingredients to suit your tastes, but be careful adding anything that would melt. Things like chocolate chips will melt when stirred into the candy coating.

Makes 6–8 servings

salted caramel corn pops balls

FORGET THE CLASSIC CARAMEL POPCORN BALLS and surprise your Halloween trick o' treaters with this twist on an old classic. With a sprinkle of salt, these babies are salty, sweet, and crunchy all at the same time.

4 tablespoons unsalted butter

1 cup packed light brown sugar

1/2 cup light corn syrup

2/3 cup sweetened condensed milk

8 cups Corn Pops

Flaky sea salt for garnish

Line a large baking sheet with parchment paper and set aside.

In a medium saucepan over medium-high heat, combine butter, brown sugar, and corn syrup. Bring to a boil and whisk in condensed milk. Continue cooking, stirring constantly until a candy thermometer reaches 235 degrees (or the soft-ball stage). Remove from heat.

Place Corn Pops in a large bowl and slowly pour caramel over top, tossing to coat. Butter hands slightly and shape into balls about 4 inches in diameter. Set on parchment paper and sprinkle tops with sea salt. Serve immediately, or store in an airtight container for up to 3 days.

Makes 14 Balls

red velvet
Rice Krispies Truffles

YES, YOU READ THAT CORRECTLY. These are red velvet Rice Krispies treats that you roll around in white chocolate. They're dangerously good.

5 tablespoons unsalted butter

3 cups mini marshmallows

1/3 cup red velvet cake mix

3 cups Rice Krispies

8 ounces white chocolate, roughly chopped

Line a large baking sheet with parchment paper and set aside.

In a large nonstick stock pot, melt butter over medium-high heat. Add marshmallows and stir until completely melted. Stir in cake mix. Remove from heat and fold in Rice Krispies until coated.

Let mixture cool for 3 minutes and form into 1-inch balls and place on prepared baking sheet. Let cool completely.

In a medium microwave-safe bowl, microwave chocolate for 1 minute and stir. If not completely melted, microwave in 15 second intervals, stirring after each until smooth.

Dip balls into melted chocolate using toothpicks or a fork and return to baking sheet. Let the chocolate coating harden on the counter for 1 hour or in the refrigerator for 20 minutes. Store in an airtight container for up to 3 days.

Makes 28 Truffles

WHITE CHOCOLATE
CHEX CLUSTERS

THIS IS ONE OF THE SIMPLEST RECIPES TO MAKE, but it sure doesn't taste that way! White chocolate, Rice Chex, and salted cashews were obviously always meant to go together.

8 ounces white chocolate, roughly chopped

5 cups Rice Chex

1 cup salted cashews

Grease a 12-cup muffin pan with butter and set aside.

In a medium microwave-safe bowl, microwave chocolate for 1 minute and stir. If not completely melted, microwave in 15 second intervals, stirring after each until smooth.

Place Rice Chex and cashews in a large bowl and slowly pour white chocolate over top, tossing to coat. Place $1/2$ cup mixture in each prepared muffin tin.

Place in refrigerator and chill for 15 minutes, or until hardened. Serve immediately, or store in an airtight container for up to 5 days.

Makes 12 clusters

CINNAMON CHEERIOS CRUNCHIES

WHILE THESE MAY SOUND STRANGE, Cinnamon Cheerios Crunchies might quite possibly be one of my favorite recipes in this book. They are absolutely addicting to eat on their own, but can be added to anything from trail mix to ice cream.

4 cups Cinnamon Cheerios

1 cup crushed Cinnamon Cheerios

1/2 cup packed brown sugar

1/2 teaspoon salt

1/2 cup unsalted butter, melted

Preheat oven to 275 degrees. Line a large baking sheet with parchment paper and set aside.

In a large bowl, toss together Cheerios, crushed Cheerios, brown sugar, and salt. Slowly pour melted butter over Cheerios mixture, tossing evenly to coat.

Spread mixture in an even layer on baking sheet and bake for 25 minutes, stirring halfway through. Let cool and serve immediately or store in an airtight container for up to 5 days.

Makes 4 cups

Date Pecan All-Bran Truffles

THESE TRUFFLES ARE PRACTICALLY HEALTH FOOD! With the protein from the pecans, the fiber from the All-Bran, and the health benefits from the honey, they might as well mark these as "diet food." Well, maybe they would if they didn't taste like candy!

1 cup All-Bran Flakes

10 pitted dates

2/3 cup chopped pecans, divided

2 tablespoons honey

2 tablespoons cream cheese

Place All-Bran Flakes, dates, 1/3 cup pecans, honey, and cream cheese in bowl of a food processor and mix until a ball forms.

Form 1 tablespoon of mixture into balls and roll in remaining chopped pecans. Store in the refrigerator in an airtight container until ready to serve.

Makes 12 Truffles

Peanut Butter Crunch
Chocolate Bark

DARK CHOCOLATE AND CAP'N CRUNCH'S PEANUT BUTTER CRUNCH join forces in this decadent candy bark. It's fun for both kids and adults, and is sure to relieve tension when you get to break apart the bark!

1 1/2 cups Cap'n Crunch's Peanut Butter Crunch, divided

11 ounces dark chocolate, chopped

Line a large baking sheet with parchment paper and set aside.

Pulse 1/2 cup Peanut Butter Crunch in a food processor until powdered. Set aside.

In a medium microwave-safe bowl, microwave chocolate for 1 minute and stir. If not completely melted, microwave in 15 second intervals, stirring after each until smooth.

Pour half of the chocolate onto prepared baking sheet. Cover chocolate with powdered Peanut Butter Crunch, leaving a 1/2-inch border around the edges. Carefully pour the remaining chocolate on top using the back of a spoon to spread to the edges. Sprinkle remaining 1 cup Peanut Butter Crunch over the top of the chocolate and press gently to make sure the cereal sticks.

Chill in refrigerator for 30 minutes, or until hardened. Break into pieces and serve immediately, or store in an airtight container for up to 3 days.

Makes 10–12 Pieces

Banana Split Cheerios Trail Mix

PLAIN OLD TRAIL MIX HAS BEEN AROUND FOR YEARS, but with a few fun additions you can have a banana split on the go. Being able to grab a bag for a quick snack, or on-the-go breakfast is exactly what the cereal gods ordered.

4 cups Banana Nut Cheerios

1 cup dried banana chips

1 cup mini marshmallows

1 cup roasted peanuts

1/2 cup Craisins

1/2 cup chocolate chips

1/2 cup caramel bits

1/2 cup dried pineapple bits

Combine all ingredients in a large bowl and store in an airtight container.

Makes 9 cups

Fiber One
Butterscotch Haystacks

WHILE THE TRADITIONAL HAYSTACKS are made with chow mien noodles, no one will notice the difference when you use Fiber One Original instead! With an added benefit of fiber, these will make you feel a lot less guilty when you eat 13 in one sitting!

1 (11-ounce) bag butterscotch morsels

3/4 cup crunchy peanut butter

3 cups Fiber One Original

2 cups mini marshmallows

Line a large baking sheet with parchment paper and set aside.

In a large microwave-safe bowl, microwave butterscotch morsels for 1 minute and stir. If not completely melted, microwave in 15 second intervals, stirring after each until smooth. Stir in peanut butter until well blended.

Add Fiber One and marshmallows, tossing to coat completely. Drop by rounded tablespoons onto parchment paper. Refrigerate until ready to serve.

Makes 28 Haystacks

cookies

Chex Chocolate Chunk
Peanut Butter Cookies

IF YOU ARE AS INDECISIVE AS I AM, then this is the cookie for you. By adding the crunch of Rice Chex to traditional peanut butter and chocolate chip cookies, you will be delighted to discover your new favorite cookie in these little babies!

1 cup flour

1 teaspoon baking soda

$1/2$ teaspoon salt

$1/2$ cup unsalted butter, room temperature

$1/2$ cup creamy peanut butter

$1/2$ cup sugar

$1/3$ cup packed brown sugar

1 egg

1 teaspoon vanilla extract

$1 1/2$ cups Rice Chex

1 cup semisweet chocolate baking chunks

Preheat oven to 350 degrees. Line a large baking sheet with parchment paper and set aside.

In a large bowl, whisk together flour, baking soda, and salt. Set aside.

In stand mixer, cream together butter, peanut butter, sugar, and brown sugar. Add egg and vanilla. Beat in flour mixture, mixing until just combined. Remove bowl from mixer and fold in Chex and chocolate chunks by hand.

Drop dough by rounded tablespoons onto prepared baking sheet and bake for 12 minutes, or until middles are set. Let cool for 5 minutes on baking sheet before transferring to a wire rack. Store in an airtight container for up to 5 days.

MAKES 24 COOKIES

FRUITY PEBBLES
Macarons

THESE FRUITY PEBBLES MACARONS are what launched this entire cookbook. I dreamed these up in 2011 and they were an instant sensation on my blog. With their bright colors and fancy French background, these little darlings are everything you ever dreamed about.

SHELLS

75 grams* powdered fruity pebbles, sifted

75 grams almond meal, sifted

200 grams powdered sugar, sifted

100 grams egg whites, room temperature

28 grams sugar

5 grams powdered dehydrated egg whites

Line 2 large baking sheets with parchment paper and set aside. In a medium bowl sift together powdered Fruity Pebbles, almond meal, and powdered sugar. Set aside.

In a stand mixer, whisk egg whites at medium-low speed. Once the egg whites begin to foam, slowly sprinkle in sugar and dehydrated egg whites. Slowly increase speed to medium-high and beat until a firm meringue forms.

Using a rubber spatula, gently fold dry ingredients into the meringue, until combined. You will have to break the meringue to do this, but do not over-stir. Transfer mixture to a pastry bag with a plain round tip and pipe 1-inch rounds onto prepared baking sheets leaving 1 inch between macarons to allow the batter to spread. Once all macarons have been piped, pick up the baking sheet with both hands and tap it firmly on the counter several times. This will remove any air bubbles. Let sit for 30 minutes to 1 hour, depending on humidity levels. The macarons are ready to bake when the tops are no longer sticky.

Preheat oven to 285 degrees.

Bake for 18–20 minutes, or until shells easily pop off the parchment paper. Remove shells immediately from baking sheet and cool on a wire rack.

Dry ingredients for the macaron shells are best measured by weight rather than volume for a superlative product.

FILLING

1/2 cup unsalted butter, room temperature

1/2 cup powdered Fruity Pebbles

1 teaspoon vanilla extract

1 cup powdered sugar

In a stand mixer, cream together butter, powdered Fruity Pebbles, and vanilla. Slowly add powdered sugar, scraping down the sides and bottom of the bowl as needed.

Transfer filling to a pastry bag with a plain round tip and pipe onto a cooled macaron shell and sandwich together with a second shell. Repeat until all shells are used. Store in an airtight container in the refrigerator for 24 hours before eating. Let warm to room temperature before serving.

Makes 24 macarons

CHOCOLATE FUDGE
RICE KRISPIES COOKIES

IF YOU LIKE A CRUNCH BAR, this is your cookie! These Chocolate Fudge Rice Krispies Cookies are a Crunch bar, in an alien cookie form. With rich chocolate and little pops of Rice Krispies, they are the perfect afternoon snack.

1/2 cup flour

1 1/2 cups powdered sugar

1/3 cup dark cocoa powder

1/4 teaspoon salt

2 egg whites

1 teaspoon vanilla extract

1 cup Rice Krispies

Preheat oven to 350 degrees. Line a large baking sheet with parchment paper and set aside.

In a large bowl, whisk together flour, powdered sugar, cocoa, and salt. Beat in egg whites and vanilla until just combined. Fold in Rice Krispies.

Drop dough by rounded tablespoons onto prepared baking sheet. Bake for 10 minutes, or until tops are set and shiny. Let cool for 10 minutes on baking sheet before transferring to a cooling rack to cool completely. Store in an airtight container for up to 5 days.

Makes 12 cookies

ROCKY ROAD CHOCOLATE CHEERIOS COOKIES

ROCKY ROAD ISN'T ONLY GREAT IN ICE CREAM FORM, it is also amazing in cookie form! With the delightful crunch you get from the Chocolate Cheerios and walnuts, these are a wonderful chocolate cookie surprise.

1 cup flour

1/3 cup dark cocoa powder

1/2 teaspoon baking soda

1/4 teaspoon salt

1/2 cup unsalted butter, room temperature

1/2 cup sugar

1/2 cup packed brown sugar

1 egg

1 teaspoon vanilla extract

1 cup mini marshmallows

1 cup Chocolate Cheerios

1/2 cup chopped walnuts

Preheat oven to 350 degrees. Line a large baking sheet with parchment paper and set aside.

In a large bowl, whisk together flour, cocoa powder, baking soda, and salt. Set aside.

In stand mixer, cream together butter, sugar, and brown sugar. Add egg and vanilla. Beat in flour mixture, mixing until just combined. Remove from stand mixer and fold in marshmallows, Cheerios, and walnuts by hand.

Drop dough by rounded tablespoons onto prepared baking sheet. Bake for 8–10 minutes, or until middles are set.

Let cool for 5 minutes on baking sheet before transferring to a cooling rack to cool completely. Store in an airtight container for up to 5 days.

Makes 24 cookies

Lucky Charms
Macarons

LUCKY CHARMS COMBINE WITH THE FRENCH MACARON to make something—magically delicious! While I may be corny, I promise you will not be disappointed when you bite into one of these Lucky Charms Macarons.

SHELLS

75 grams* powdered Lucky Charms cereal
    (excluding marshmallows), sifted

75 grams almond meal, sifted

200 grams powdered sugar, sifted

100 grams egg whites, room temperature

28 grams sugar

5 grams powdered dehydrated egg whites

Line 2 large baking sheets with parchment paper and set aside. In a medium bowl sift together powdered Lucky Charms, almond meal, and powdered sugar. Set aside.

In a stand mixer, whisk egg whites at medium-low speed. Once the egg whites begin to foam, slowly sprinkle in sugar and dehydrated egg whites. Slowly increase speed to medium-high and beat until a firm meringue forms.

Using a rubber spatula, gently fold dry ingredients into the meringue, until combined. You will have to break the meringue to do this, but do not over-stir. Transfer mixture to a pastry bag with a plain round tip and pipe 1-inch rounds onto prepared baking sheets, leaving 1 inch between macarons to allow the batter to spread. Once all macarons have been piped, pick up the baking sheet with both hands and tap it firmly on the counter several times. This will remove any air bubbles. Let sit for 30 minutes to 1 hour, depending on humidity levels. The macarons are ready to bake when the tops are no longer sticky.

Preheat oven to 285 degrees.

Bake for 18–20 minutes, or until shells easily pop off the parchment paper. Remove shells immediately from baking sheet and cool on a wire rack.

Dry ingredients for the macaron shells are best measured by weight rather than volume for a superlative product.

FILLING

1/2 cup unsalted butter, room temperature

1 teaspoon vanilla extract

2 cups marshmallow creme

1 cup powdered sugar

24 Lucky Charms marshmallows, for garnish

In a stand mixer, cream together butter and vanilla. Add the marshmallow creme, mixing until smooth. Slowly add powdered sugar, scraping down the sides and bottom of the bowl as needed.

Transfer filling to a pastry bag with a plain round tip and pipe onto a cooled macaron shell and sandwich together with a second shell. Pipe a small dot of filling on top of macaron and press a Lucky Charms marshmallow into it. Repeat until all shells are used. Store in an airtight container, in the refrigerator for 24 hours before eating. Let warm to room temperature before serving.

Makes 24 macarons

APPLE JACKS
COOKIES

IMAGINE THAT A SUGAR COOKIE AND A SNICKERDOODLE GOT MARRIED and had a baby named Apple Jacks. Then they all joined forces and made one big cookie. This is that cookie.

2 cups Apple Jacks, divided

1 1/4 cups flour

1 teaspoon baking powder

1/2 teaspoon baking soda

1/4 teaspoon salt

1/2 cup unsalted butter, room temperature

3/4 cup sugar

1 egg

1/2 teaspoon vanilla extract

Preheat oven to 350 degrees. Line 2 baking sheets with parchment paper and set aside.

In a food processor, puree 1/2 cup Apple Jacks until fine. Place powdered Apple Jacks in a small bowl and set aside. In a medium bowl, whisk together flour, baking powder, baking soda, and salt. Set aside.

In a large bowl, cream together butter and sugar until light and fluffy. Add egg and vanilla, stirring to combine. Beat in flour mixture until a soft dough forms. Fold in remaining 1 1/2 cups Apple Jacks.

Roll 1 heaping tablespoon of dough into a ball and coat with powdered Apple Jacks. Place on baking sheet, leaving room for spreading. Continue with rest of dough. Bake for 13–15 minutes, or until lightly browned around edges. Remove from oven and let rest for 5 minutes on baking sheet. Transfer to wire rack and let cool completely. Serve immediately or store in an airtight container.

MAKES 16 COOKIES

Cap'n Crunch Cookies

IMAGINE REACHING INTO YOUR GRANDMOTHER'S COOKIE JAR and finding a big surprise; a Cap'n Crunch Cookie! With crispy edges and chunks of Cap'n Crunch, these aren't your traditional cookie jar cookie.

$1^1/_2$ cups Cap'n Crunch, divided

1 cup flour

$^3/_4$ teaspoon baking soda

$^1/_4$ teaspoon salt

$^1/_2$ cup unsalted butter, room temperature

$^1/_4$ cup sugar

$^1/_4$ cup packed light brown sugar

1 egg

1 teaspoon vanilla extract

Preheat oven to 350 degrees. Line 2 baking sheets with parchment paper and set aside.

In a food processor, puree $^3/_4$ cup Cap'n Crunch until fine. In a medium bowl, whisk together powdered Cap'n Crunch, flour, baking soda, and salt. Set aside.

In a large bowl, cream together butter, sugar, and brown sugar until light and fluffy. Add egg and vanilla, stirring to combine. Beat in flour mixture until a soft dough forms. Fold in remaining $^3/_4$ cup Cap'n Crunch.

Roll 1 heaping tablespoon of dough into a ball and place on prepared baking sheet, leaving room for spreading. Continue with rest of dough. Bake for 10–12 minutes or until lightly browned around edges. Remove from oven and let rest for 5 minutes on baking sheet. Transfer to wire rack and let cool completely. Serve immediately or store in an airtight container.

Makes 16 cookies

Cinnamon Toast Crunch Macarons

WHILE THIS CLASSIC FRENCH COOKIE may be a wee bit snooty, it's perfect for any occasion when made with Cinnamon Toast Crunch!

SHELLS

75 grams* powdered Cinnamon
    Toast Crunch, sifted

75 grams almond meal, sifted

200 grams powdered sugar, sifted

100 grams egg whites, room temperature

28 grams sugar

5 grams powdered dehydrated egg whites

Line 2 large baking sheets with parchment paper and set aside. In a medium bowl sift together powdered Cinnamon Toast Crunch, almond meal, and powdered sugar. Set aside.

In a stand mixer, whisk egg whites at medium-low speed. Once the egg whites begin to foam, slowly sprinkle in sugar and dehydrated egg whites. Slowly increase speed to medium-high and beat until a firm meringue forms.

Using a rubber spatula, gently fold dry ingredients into the meringue, until combined. You will have to break the meringue to do this, but do not over-stir. Transfer mixture to a pastry bag with a plain round tip and pipe 1-inch rounds onto prepared baking sheets, leaving 1 inch between macarons to allow the batter to spread. Once all macarons have been piped, pick up the baking sheet with both hands and tap it firmly on the counter several times. This will remove any air bubbles. Let sit for 30 minutes to 1 hour, depending on humidity levels. The macarons are ready to bake when the tops are no longer sticky.

Preheat oven to 285 degrees.

Bake for 18–20 minutes, or until shells easily pop off the parchment paper. Remove shells immediately from baking sheet and cool on a wire rack.

Dry ingredients for the macaron shells are best measured by weight rather than volume for a superlative product.

FILLING

1/2 cup unsalted butter, room temperature

1 teaspoon vanilla extract

1 1/2 cups powdered sugar

1 teaspoon cinnamon

24 Cinnamon Toast Crunch pieces, for garnish

In a stand mixer, cream together butter and vanilla. Slowly add powdered sugar and cinnamon, scraping down the sides and bottom of the bowl as needed.

Transfer filling to a pastry bag with a plain round tip and pipe onto a cooled macaron shell and sandwich together with a second shell. Pipe a small dot of filling on top of macaron and press a Cinnamon Toast Crunch piece into it. Repeat until all shells are used. Store in an airtight container in the refrigerator for 24 hours before eating. Let warm to room temperature before serving.

Makes 24 macarons

Frozen Treats

COOKIE CRISPS COOKIE DOUGH ICE CREAM SANDWICHES

IF YOU HAVE KIDS THAT LIKE ICE CREAM (and really, what kid doesn't love ice cream?), this is the perfect fun recipe to make together. With a little adult help, they will be on their way to making their very own ice cream sandwiches!

6 ounces semisweet chocolate,
roughly chopped

3/4 cup Cookie Crisps

1 pint cookie dough ice cream

Line a large baking sheet with parchment paper and set aside.

In a medium microwave-safe bowl, microwave chocolate for 1 minute and stir. If not completely melted, microwave in 15 second intervals, stirring after each until smooth.

Pour 1 heaping tablespoon of chocolate onto parchment paper and spread into a 3-inch diameter circle. Press 6–7 Cookie Crisps pieces into chocolate. Continue until all the chocolate has been used. Chill in refrigerator for 20 minutes, or until completely hardened.

To assemble the sandwiches, put a large scoop of slightly-softened ice cream between two chocolate pieces and press together lightly. Once all sandwiches are assembled, place in freezer for at least 30 minutes to firm up. Serve immediately or wrap individually with plastic wrap and keep in freezer in an airtight container until ready to serve.

Makes 4 servings

Cap'n Crunch
MILKSHAKE

CEREAL AND MILK HAVE ALWAYS BEEN BEST FRIENDS, but they usually come in a bowl and are not frozen. This Cap'n Crunch Milkshake is the frozen version of your favorite breakfast combination!

2 cups Cap'n Crunch

1 1/2 cups vanilla ice cream

1/4 cup whole milk

Whipped cream for garnish

Combine Cap'n Crunch, ice cream, and milk in blender. Blend until smooth. Pour into a chilled glass and top with a spoonful of whipped cream.

Quick Tip: Having a powerful blender is very important for a smooth milkshake. If your blender is only so-so, puree the Cap'n Crunch into a fine powder before adding the remaining ingredients.

Makes 1 serving

FRUIT LOOPS POPSICLES

HOW CAN YOUR LIFE EVER BE COMPLETE if you have never had a Popsicle made with cereal? It just can't! Try these out with Fruit Loops as seen, or substitute with your personal favorite cereal.

3 cups Fruit Loops, divided

2 cups milk

1 cup heavy cream

3 egg yolks

1/3 cup sugar

2 teaspoons vanilla extract

In a large bowl, stir together 2 cups Fruit Loops, milk, and cream. Let soak for 30 minutes, stirring occasionally. Strain out cereal and discard.

In a large saucepan over medium-high heat, whisk together cereal milk, egg yolks, sugar, and vanilla. Bring to a boil, stirring constantly. Remove from heat and cool in the refrigerator until cold to the touch.

Divide remaining 1 cup Fruit Loops among Popsicle molds. Pour cooled milk mixture into molds and insert Popsicle sticks. Freeze for at least 6 hours.

MAKES 10 POPSICLES

Honey Bunches of Oats
Fried Ice Cream

THE IDEA OF FRIED ICE CREAM has always confused me. Do they actually fry it? Why isn't it a melted mess when it's served? And how is it so delicious? Once I learned that you could make it with Honey Bunches of Oats, there was no turning back!

3 cups Honey Bunches of Oats

1/4 cup packed brown sugar

1/4 teaspoon salt

5 tablespoons unsalted butter, melted

4 cups cinnamon ice cream

Honey, for garnish

Preheat oven to 275 degrees. Line a large baking sheet with parchment paper and set aside.

In a large bowl, toss together Honey Bunches of Oats, brown sugar, and salt. Slowly pour melted butter over mixture, tossing evenly to coat.

Spread mixture in an even layer on baking sheet. Bake for 15 minutes, stirring half way through baking. Remove from oven and let cool completely.

Form ice cream balls with hands, using 1 cup of ice cream per ball. Immediately roll in Honey Bunches of Oats mixture, pressing lightly. Serve immediately with a drizzle of honey on top.

Makes 4 servings

corn pops
ice cream

THIS IS A PERFECT "make it your own" recipe. I love the flavor Corn Pops gives to the ice cream, but that doesn't mean you shouldn't try this formula out with your favorite type of cereal. Give it a shot with Trix, Apple Jacks, or Waffle Crisp! The flavor opportunities are endless, and scrumptious.

2 cups milk

1 cup heavy cream

3 cups Corn Pops

3/4 cup sugar

1 teaspoon vanilla extract

In a large bowl, stir together milk, cream, and Corn Pops. Let soak for 30 minutes, stirring occasionally. Strain out cereal and discard.

Transfer milk mixture to a large saucepan and whisk in sugar. Bring to a boil, stirring constantly. Boil for 2 minutes and remove from heat. Stir in vanilla. Cool mixture in the refrigerator until cold to the touch.

Once cooled, transfer mixture to your ice cream maker and mix according to manufacture instructions. Ice cream will be in the soft serve stage at this point. To harden, transfer to an airtight container and freeze for at least 3 hours.

Makes 6 servings

cocoa pebbles
ice cream sandwiches

THERE IS NOTHING BETTER on a hot summer day than an ice cream sandwich—well unless the ice cream sandwich is made with Cocoa Pebbles!

4 tablespoons unsalted butter

3 cups mini marshmallows

3 cups Cocoa Pebbles

1 pint ice cream

Grease a standard-size muffin pan with a small amount of butter and set aside.

In a large nonstick stock pot, melt butter over medium-high heat. Add marshmallows, stirring until completely melted. Remove from heat and fold in Cocoa Pebbles.

Press 2 heaping tablespoons Cocoa Pebbles mixture into each muffin cup. Let cool completely and remove.

To assemble the sandwiches, put a large scoop of slightly softened ice cream between two halves and press together lightly. Once all sandwiches are assembled, place in freezer for at least 30 minutes to firm up. Serve immediately or wrap individually with plastic wrap and keep in freezer in an airtight container until ready to serve.

Makes 6 servings

I would like to dedicate this book to anyone who has ever eaten Cap'n Crunch for breakfast, lunch, and dinner. You are my kind of people. —*J. S.*

First Edition
17 16 15 14 13   5 4 3 2 1

Text © 2013 Jessica Segarra
Photographs © 2013 Jessica Segarra

Published by
Gibbs Smith
P.O. Box 667
Layton, Utah 84041

1.800.835.4993 orders
www.gibbs-smith.com

Designed by Katie Jennings
Printed and bound in China

Gibbs Smith books are printed on either recycled, 100% post-consumer waste, FSC-certified papers or on paper produced from sustainable PEFC-certified forest/controlled wood source. Learn more at www.pefc.org.

Library of Congress Cataloging-in-Publication Data

Segarra, Jessica.
  Cereal sweets & treats / written and photographed by Jessica Segarra. —
First edition.
      pages cm
  title: Cereal sweets and treats
  ISBN 978-1-4236-3215-3
1. Cooking (Cereals) 2. Breakfast cereals. 3. Cereals, Prepared. I. Title. II.
Title: Cereal sweets and treats.
  TX808.S44 2013
  641.3'31—dc23
                                        2012050557

METRIC CONVERSION CHART

VOLUME MEASUREMENTS

U.S.	METRIC
1 teaspoon	5 ml
1 tablespoon	15 ml
1/4 cup	60 ml
1/3 cup	75 ml
1/2 cup	125 ml
2/3 cup	150 ml
3/4 cup	175 ml
1 cup	250 ml

WEIGHT MEASUREMENTS

U.S.	METRIC
1/2 ounce	15 g
1 ounce	30 g
3 ounces	90 g
4 ounces	115 g
8 ounces	225 g
12 ounces	350 g
1 pound	450 g
2 1/4 pounds	1 kg

TEMPERATURE CONVERSION

FAHRENHEIT	CELSIUS
250	120
300	150
325	160
350	180
375	190
400	200
425	220
450	230